Favorite
Appliqué & Embroidery Quilts

Betty Alderman

American Quilter's Society
P. O. Box 3290 • Paducah, KY 42002-3290
www.AQSquilt.com

Located in Paducah, Kentucky, the American Quilter's Society (AQS) is dedicated to promoting the accomplishments of today's quilters. Through its publications and events, AQS strives to honor today's quiltmakers and their work and to inspire future creativity and innovation in quiltmaking.

EDITOR: BARBARA SMITH
GRAPHIC DESIGN: ELAINE WILSON
COVER DESIGN: MICHAEL BUCKINGHAM
PHOTOGRAPHY: CHARLES R. LYNCH

Library of Congress Cataloging-in-Publication Data
Alderman, Betty
    Favorite applique and embroidery quilts / by Betty Alderman.
       p. cm.
    ISBN 1-57432-839-5
    1. Quilting.   2. Patchwork.   I. Title.

    TT835.A425 2004
    746.46'041--dc22

                        2003027999

Additional copies of this book may be ordered from the American Quilter's Society, PO Box 3290, Paducah, KY 42002-3290; 800-626-5420 (orders only please); or online at www.AQSquilt.com. For all other inquiries, call 270-898-7903.

Dedication

To my granddaughters, Jessica and Abby—this book is for you.

Acknowledgments

Without my family and friends, I could never make quilts and write about them.

I am indebted to my husband, Fred, for his broad shoulders and unerring eye. Those special qualities make my life easier, and I rely on them every day.

My daughter, Betsy, cheerfully answers all my computer questions and has helped me gather up all the loose ends for this book. Thank you, Betsy.

My Thursday stitching friends are huge supporters of me and of each other. What a group! Thank you Carol, Helene, Carroll, Jane, Katie, Lou, and Nancy. Thursday is the best day of the week for me.

To my quilting friends in Arizona, I just want to give you all a big hug! Even though I left there five years ago, you continue to be my dear friends and help-mates. There are so many of you that I can't name you all here, but you know who you are. I am forever grateful to Laurene Sinema and her Quilted Apple shop. Without her, we would never have connected.

Soon after I had surgery several years ago, Diane Ebner offered to machine quilt some of my quilt tops so I might have them ready for Quilt Market. We have had a wonderful working relationship ever since. Diane and my friend Val Sparks have recently opened their own shop in Phoenix, Arizona, called Bernina Connection.

To Dorothy and Linda at the Mendon Village Quilt Shop, thank you for allowing me to come to your shop and mess up all your fabric as I look for just the right combination. Whenever I need a break, I love to visit you.

I owe such a debt of gratitude to Meredith Schroeder and all the AQS staff—Barbara Smith, Helen Squire, and all the others—for allowing me to be part of your group of authors. Thank you for your guidance and support. It has been an experience I shall treasure always.

Contents

Preface

Appliqué has always been my favorite form of quiltmaking. The preciseness of piecework can certainly be satisfying, but appliqué offers a freedom that knows no boundaries. My early training was in drawing and painting, but once I learned to transfer my designs onto fabric and apply them to a background, I was hooked forever.

Like most devotees of appliqué, I work with 100 percent cotton fabric. The exciting colors, the imaginative prints, and the smooth, cool, tactile quality of cotton has made it my medium of choice for many years.

Whether you are an appliqué enthusiast or you are just testing the waters, I ask you to join me in an adventure. We will cut, press, appliqué, and embroider to our hearts' content. A lifelong passion for this form of quiltmaking will surely be your reward.

Introduction

This book features several projects that are made with fusible web and embellished with simple embroidery. The appliqué in these projects has been done with a lightweight, paper-backed fusible web. The stitching around the outside edge of the fused appliqué can be done by hand or machine. Directions are given for the stitching according to the way the original quilt was made. However, as the quiltmaker, you may choose either method to finish the edges of your appliqué.

Two of the quilts do not incorporate appliqué at all but are examples of the ever-popular redwork and bluework. CRAZY FOR BLUEWORK is a crazy quilt adorned with whimsical bluework designs, and HEARTS AND FLOWERS is a pretty floral wallhanging stitched in redwork surrounded by an unusual floral border. The designs on these two quilts are done in simple outline embroidery. This same stitch is also evident on all the other quilts, giving them added decorative dimension and giving you the pleasure of adding fine handwork to your quilts.

REDWORK BEAUTY and BLUEWORK AND BEYOND were inspired by designs found on coverlets woven on Jacquard looms during the nineteenth century. They may look complicated, but I promise you that they are easy to make. You will surely impress your family and friends with these lovely motifs inspired by weavers from the past.

While based on traditional album quilts, CHERRY BERRY ALBUM, FUNKY FOLK ART RED-WORK, and JUST MY DOODLES have a playful look achieved by redesigning and using updated color-ways. Here is your chance to use all those glorious brights you have in your fabric collection.

Three of the quilts are composed of a single block design. MAY BASKET has one block set on point, while BLUE TULIPS and A "TOUCH" OF HOME feature a single block repeated several times in different configurations. I encourage you to play around with the settings of these blocks to create other wonderful design possibilities.

THE APRON BRIGADE place mat will give you a taste of the fun you can have coloring designs on paper and transferring them onto fabric by using a color copier or your computer scanner.

I hope you can hardly wait to get started!

Supplies to Have on Hand

The following information will give you a detailed description of the type and quality of supplies needed to complete the projects in this book. In addition, the directions for each quilt include the materials for that particular project. I cannot stress enough the importance of working with good materials and tools. You will be devoting your precious time to making a quilt that you will want to display in your home or to give to a special person in your life. Only by using the very best will you be able to do your very best.

Fabric

A visit to your local quilt shop will provide you with a selection of the best 100 percent cotton fabrics. The staff works with fabric every day, and they are skilled at putting colors and prints together in a pleasing way. They will work with you, suggesting possible combinations until you are happy with your fabric choices.

The quilts in this book are all designed to be wallhangings. Unless you plan to use your quilt as a bed covering or crib quilt, it is not really necessary to wash your fabrics before you use them. If you are more comfortable washing your fabrics first, by all means do so, but you have my permission to skip this step and get right to the fun part!

Fusible Web

All of the appliqué directions in this book call for lightweight, paper-backed fusible web. This is a product available in most fabric stores. I want to emphasize that you must be sure you are buying lightweight and paperbacked fusible web. Nothing else will do.

Thread

I have used DMC® embroidery floss for the embroidery on all of the quilts in this book. Occasionally, in a class, I am asked if the color red will run. I have tested it again and again and have never had a problem.

A few of these quilts have been hand quilted. I used 100 percent cotton quilting thread in some instances and DMC Pearl Cotton where noted.

The majority of the quilts were quilted on a sewing machine. The thread of choice on top was clear, monofilament thread, and cotton thread was used in the bobbin.

Tools to Complete Your Projects

+ Zigzag sewing machine in good working order

+ Embroidery needles, size 7 or 8

+ Embroidery scissors

+ Sharp 8" scissors for cutting fusible web and appliqué designs (The new theory is that paper will not dull scissors. My experience says it is true!)

+ Thimble

+ #4 extra hard pencil and/or fine-line, permanent pen for marking embroidery lines on fabric

+ #2 pencil for tracing appliqué designs onto fusible web designs

+ Light box (optional)

+ Embroidery hoop (optional)

General Instructions

"Please read through all of the pattern's directions before you begin to cut or sew." When teaching a class, my students always laugh when I read that sentence to them. No one is very good at following that simple direction, but it is so important. By taking the time to do that one thing, we can all save ourselves the grief of being confused as we progress through the quiltmaking process.

Every effort has been made to make these directions as clear and precise as possible, but it is assumed that the quiltmaker is familiar with basic quiltmaking skills. If you are a beginning quiltmaker, there are some books listed in the Suggested Reading section on page 94 which will be helpful in perfecting your skills.

All seam allowances are ¼" and are included in the cutting measurements. The lengths given for the borders and sashings are the ideal measurements. Individual quilts may vary. Therefore it is a good idea to measure your quilt as you piece it together to determine the exact length you need to cut your borders and sashings.

Directions for Appliqué

1. Before you begin, read all of the directions noted below and those included with the fusible web.

2. With your #2 pencil, trace each design element onto the paper side of the fusible web. Leave at least ½" between each design element. If the design is asymmetrical, you will need to make a reverse pattern. This will prevent your appliqué from being backward.

3. Cut out the designs, leaving ¼" beyond the drawn designs.

4. Set your dry iron to the silk/wool setting. If your iron is too hot, your fusible web will not adhere to the fabric.

5. Press each design onto the wrong side of the fabric you have chosen for that particular design. Press for about five seconds.

6. Cut out the design on the drawn line. Important: Keep your edges very smooth.

7. Prepare your background piece by pressing and cutting to size. I always cut my background a little larger than called for, because the appliqué and stitching may shrink the background slightly. Trim to size after the appliqué and stitching on the block is complete.

8. Peel the paper backing from the appliqué designs. When you have peeled the paper off, the fabric should have a shiny look. Place the shiny or wrong side of the appliqué onto the background. Use your pattern as a guide. Check to make sure every piece is positioned the way you want it to look. Only a very scant overlap is needed for pieces that should be placed in front of the others.

9. Press the pieces for five seconds. Turn the block over and press again for five seconds.

10. Referring to your pattern, stitch around the exposed edges of the appliqué. See the sections on Hand Embroidery Hints (this page) and Machine Appliqué Advice (page 11).

Transferring Embroidery Designs

After your appliqué is complete, you will transfer the embroidery details onto the background fabric so that they can be embroidered. There are several ways to transfer your designs onto fabric:

Tracing with pencil or pen. Place your background fabric face up over your design. In most cases you will be able to see the design through the light background fabric. Trace the design, using your #4 extra-hard pencil or your fine-line permanent pen. The advantage of the pencil is that it can be erased if you make a mistake. However, if you are working on a large project, such as REDWORK BEAUTY, the pencil marks tend to wear away before you are finished sewing. This will necessitate marking as you go along. The advantage of the pen is that it is permanent and easier to use on some fabrics that have a less than smooth surface. Important: Permanent pen markings must be heat set.

Light box method. If you have trouble seeing the design through the background fabric you may want to use a light box. You will need to make a photocopy of the design you want to transfer to the background fabric. Permission is granted to photocopy these designs for the purpose of transferring the designs onto fabric for your own personal use.

+ Make a copy of the design you want to trace onto the background fabric.

+ Place the copy on the light box and place the background fabric on top of the tracing.

+ Trace the design with the permanent pen or the #4 extra-hard pencil.

+ Heat-set the permanent pen tracing.

Hand Embroidery Hints

+ Always wash your hands before you begin to stitch.

+ If you are using a hoop, be sure to remove it whenever you put your work aside. Otherwise you may get a ring on your work, which will be difficult to remove when your work is finished.

+ Work with about 18" of thread or floss. If you try to work with more than that, your thread will become tangled and it will fray.

+ If you are using six-strand embroidery floss, strip one strand at a time from the 18" length, as shown in figure 1. To do this, grasp the length of floss with your left thumb and forefinger near the top of the strand. With your right thumb and forefinger, grasp one strand and pull up, separating it from the rest of the strands. Repeat with the number of strands you will be using.

+ Eliminate all knots in your embroidery by using the waste knot method shown in figure 2 (see Waste Knot Method, page 11).

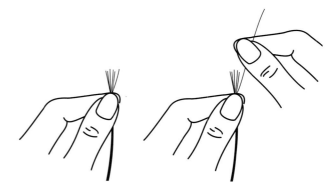

Fig. 1. **Separating strands of floss**

✤ When starting a new thread, weave it under the previous threads on the back and do the same when you are finished.

✤ Do not allow your thread to travel more than ¼" on the back, because your dark thread may show through on the front of your work. Instead, you can run your thread through the stitches on the back to get to your new starting place, or make a new waste knot and start at the new place.

WASTE KNOT METHOD

❋ Thread your embroidery needle with the required number of strands and make a knot.

❋ With your needle on top of your work, stab the needle into the right side of your fabric about 2" away from your starting point.

❋ Bring the needle up from the wrong side to the right side at the starting point and start to embroider.

❋ When you are finished with this thread, weave it through several stitches on the back and clip it off.

❋ Now cut away the knot that is on top and thread the needle with the 2" of thread. Weave this thread through several stitches on the back and clip off the remaining thread.

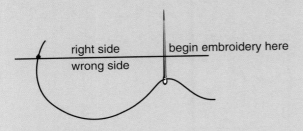

right side
wrong side
begin embroidery here

Fig. 2. Waste knot

Machine Appliqué Advice

Although it is possible to finish all of the appliqué quilts in this book with machine stitching, the BLUE TULIPS quilt is the only one that is actually machine appliquéd. The appliqué on this quilt can also be finished by hand. The choice is yours.

Quite often, it is the mood I am in or the time I have to complete a project that determines what method I use. Some people like to work only with a machine, and others are dyed-in-the-wool hand stitchers. That is the beauty of fusible web. It allows you to have a choice.

If you choose to stitch your appliqué on the machine, here are some suggestions to make the process go more smoothly:

✤ Before you begin, make sure your machine is clean and in good running order. Dust around the bobbin case and feed dogs.

✤ Replace the old needle with a new needle.

✤ Select the stitch you will be using. It will probably be a zigzag or a buttonhole stitch.

✤ Choose from the variety of threads on the market. You may want to experiment with several until you find the look you want to achieve.

✤ Fill several bobbins with a lightweight thread that matches the thread you will be using on top.

✤ Make a simple sample before you begin. This will help you find the right tension, stitch length, and width. You will also find out whether you need to place a stabilizer underneath your work. Machines vary, as do stitches, when it comes to stabilizers. Some need it, some don't. If your work is puckering, you probably need to use a stabilizer. Paper toweling works well. Simply place it between the fabric block and the feed dogs. Remove it when your stitching is complete.

✛ Whichever stitch you choose, your needle will swing from side to side. On one swing it must catch the appliqué fabric, and on the other swing it must catch the background fabric.

✛ Machine appliqué is like any decorative stitching, whether by hand or machine. It takes practice and patience to perfect the work, but the result is so gratifying. There are many good books available devoted to the fine art of machine appliqué. See the Suggested Reading section on page 94 for a listing.

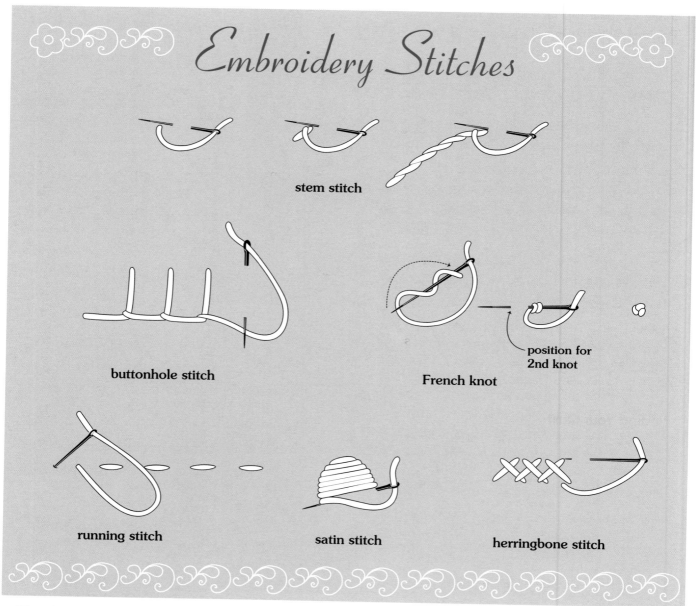

stem stitch

buttonhole stitch

French knot

position for 2nd knot

running stitch

satin stitch

herringbone stitch

Fig. 3. Embroidery stitches

Finishing Your Quilt

After your quilt top is complete, press it face down on a well-padded surface. Check to see that, wherever possible, the seam allowances are pressed toward the darker fabric. Check for stray, dark threads that will show through and make you crazy after the quilt is basted and ready to be quilted.

Make a sandwich of your quilt top by laying the backing out, face down, on a large flat surface. Layer the batting on top of the backing. Place the quilt top face up on top of the batting. Backing and batting should extend beyond the top at least 2" all around.

Baste the three layers together by using extra long stitches, or pin with rustproof safety pins. Basting spray is also an option. I find it works well on small projects that are to be machine quilted.

Quilting Suggestions

At the end of the directions for each of the quilts, there is a paragraph telling you how that particular quilt was quilted. These are only suggestions, because many of you will have your own ideas about how to quilt your project. I urge you, though, to give your quilt the finish it deserves. Machine quilting is as accepted today as hand quilting. Be creative with your quilting. Try designing your own motifs, try new threads, and remember, it's okay to quilt right over the embroidery stitches. Our grandmothers did.

Binding Your Quilt

Yardage is given in each supply list for binding.

+ Cut or make two strips, 1⅛" x the width of the quilt, plus 5".

+ Cut or make two strips, 1⅛" x the length of the quilt, plus 5".

+ Center the binding on the sides of the quilt, right sides together and the raw edges matching. The strips will extend about 2½" beyond the top and bottom of the quilt.

+ Start stitching ¼" in from the top of the quilt and stitch to within ¼" of the bottom.

+ Repeat until all four strips have been sewn to the edges of the quilt. Miter the corners according to your method of choice, or refer to the sidebar on Mitered Corners for Binding, page 14.

+ Turn the binding to the back of the quilt. Turn under ¼" and whipstitch the folded edge (fig. 4) to the back of the quilt.

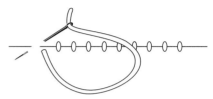

Fig. 4. Whipstitch

Making a Label

It is important to label your quilt, for several reasons. Have you ever looked through an old photo album and wondered about all those people who are preserved for posterity but who shall forever remain nameless? Frustrating, isn't it? As any quilt collector can tell you, it is equally frustrating to find a beautiful quilt painstakingly stitched by an anonymous maker. Even the humblest of quilts leaves us wondering about the woman or man who made it, because each quilt carries with it some aspect that is unique to that quilt and its maker.

If you plan to enter your quilt in a quilt show, you will be asked to label your quilt with specific information. Anytime your quilt leaves your hands to be photographed or displayed, you will want it to be properly labeled.

Having said all that, the label I place on the back of my quilts is usually fairly simple. The reason is that, once I finish a quilt, I am anxious to get back to working on my unfinished projects or to start a new one I have been planning. Making a label is something I know I must do, but keeping it simple is the way I get it done.

MITERED CORNERS FOR BINDING

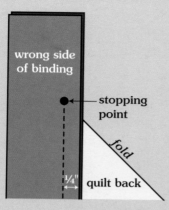

Fig. 5. Turn the seam allowances toward the quilt back and press. Fold the quilt with the binding edges right sides together.

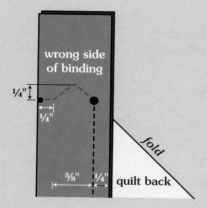

Fig. 6. Sew as shown.

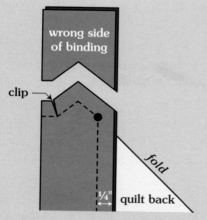

Fig. 7. Cut off the excess binding and clip the seam allowance.

This is how I make the labels for my quilts:

+ Cut a rectangle 4½" x 3½" from light background fabric. The size is optional and depends on the amount of information you want to include.

+ Iron a rectangle of freezer paper, cut the same size as the fabric, onto the back of the fabric rectangle.

+ Write all the pertinent information you want to include on the fabric side of the rectangle with a black permanent pen. Heat-set with a medium-hot iron.

+ Remove the freezer paper and turn the edges of the label (¼") to the back. Press.

+ Pin the label in place on the back. I like to place my label in the center at the bottom, but quiltmaking convention says to place it at the lower left-hand corner. If you are planning on sending your quilt to a contest or show, check the contest rules.

+ After the label is in position, thread an embroidery needle with one or two strands of embroidery floss. Choose a color that was used in your quilt. If you can't decide, black always works well.

+ Do a running stitch (see Embroidery Stitches on page 12) close to the edge of the label, securing it to the quilt back. Be sure your stitches do not show on the front of the quilt.

This is a quick and easy way to label your quilts. You may have your own favorite method—just be sure to do it. Your beautiful quilt deserves to have its own identification, and you deserve credit for creating it!

Favorite

Appliqué & Embroidery Projects

Redwork Beauty

Appliqué and embroidery quilt, 35" x 35", designed and made by the author. Betty was inspired by a nineteenth-century Jacquard coverlet.

In my hometown of Palmyra, New York, there is a museum devoted to the beautiful woven coverlets made during the nineteenth century. The weavers lived mainly in the northeast and central states east of the Mississippi. Woven coverlets differ from quilts in that they are hand woven on looms. A Jacquard-type loom was used to make the fancy two-, three-, and sometimes four-colored coverlets, many with large central medallions and intricate borders. The inspiration for this quilt came from these striking woven coverlets.

REDWORK BEAUTY
Quilt size 35" x 35"

Supply List

NOTE: Yardage is based on fabric that is at least 40" wide. Cut borders selvage to selvage.

1¼ yd. light background

Fat quarter (18" x 22") red print for center medallion

¾ yd. second red print for cornucopias, four small flowers, inner border, and binding

¼ yd. third red print for cornucopias

¼ yd. reproduction, pink-on-pink print for flowers

½ yd. red and white shirting-type fabric for outer border

2 yds. lightweight, paper-backed fusible web

10 skeins DMC floss: red 498 or 321

39" x 39" batting

39" x 39" backing

Cutting Measurements

I always cut my background a little larger than called for because the appliqué and stitching may shrink the background slightly. Trim the pieces to size after the stitching is complete.

Center block (light background)
1 square 18" x 18"

Side panels (light background)
4 rectangles 7½" x 18"

Corner blocks (light background)
4 squares 7½" x 7½"

Inner border (second red print)
4 strips 1" x 40"

Outer border (red and white shirting)
4 strips 1¾" x 40"

Binding (second red print)
4 strips 1⅛ x 40"

Directions

1. Using fusible web, appliqué the REDWORK BEAUTY center medallion design on page 20 onto the center block.

2. Buttonhole stitch around the outside edges of the medallion with two strands of floss. Do a herringbone stitch around the inside cutouts of the design.

3. Transfer the embroidery designs on pages 20–21 onto the quilt center and the background of the center block.

4. Complete the designs with a stem stitch, with two strands of floss.

5. Appliqué and embroider the side panels and the corner blocks (pp. 21–22) in the same manner as the center block. *Note: Two of the corner blocks are reversed.*

6. Piece the center block, the side panels, and the corner blocks together, according to the quilt layout shown in figure 8.

7. Stitch one inner border strip to one outer border strip along the long edge. Press the seam allowances toward the darker strip. Repeat with the other border strips.

8. Center the borders on the edges of the quilt center. Stitch the borders right sides together to

Fig. 8. REDWORK BEAUTY **quilt layout**

MITERED CORNERS

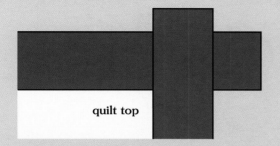

Fig 9. With the quilt right side up, turn the seam allowances toward the quilt top.

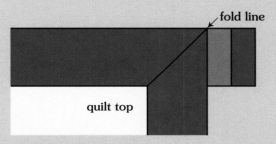

Fig. 10. Fold the top border strip at a 45-degree angle, right sides together, pressing the fold to make a distinct line.

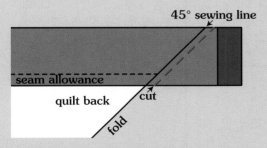

Fig. 11. Fold the quilt top in half so the border edges are right sides together. Sew on the 45-degree fold line. Cut away the excess border ¼" from the sewing line.

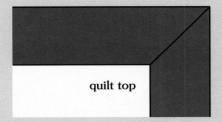

Fig. 12. Fold back and press the mitered corner.

within ¼" of the end of the quilt edges. (A 5" mitering allowance is included in the border measurement.)

9. Miter the corners according to your method of choice, or refer to the sidebar.

10. Refer to the Finishing Your Quilt section (pages 13–14) for further instructions on quilting, binding, and labeling your quilt.

Quilting Suggestions

REDWORK BEAUTY was hand quilted diagonally from the center, 2" apart, using ecru DMC Pearl Cotton thread #8. There is a heart quilted in each corner of the center block.

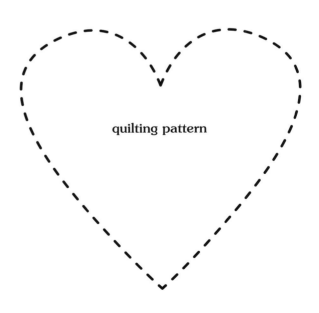

center medallion
embroidery pattern

Trace and flip the designs
to complete the pattern.

center medallion

¼ pattern

center

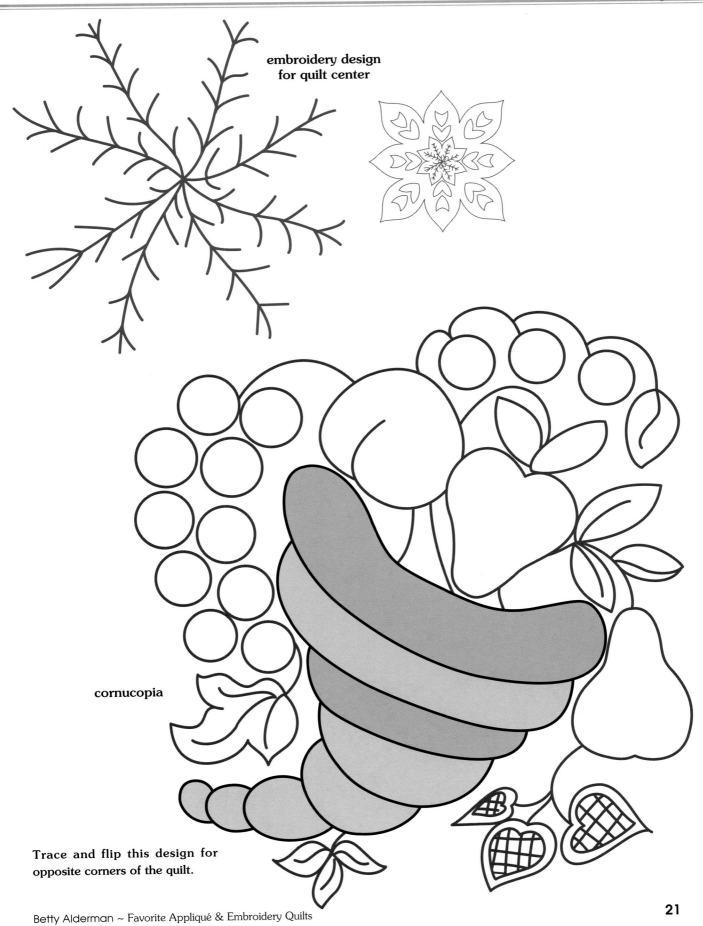

embroidery design
for quilt center

cornucopia

**Trace and flip this design for
opposite corners of the quilt.**

Trace and flip the design to complete the pattern.

½ side panel appliqué and embroidery

Favorite Appliqué & Embroidery Quilts ~ Betty Alderman

Bluework & Beyond

Appliqué and embroidery quilt, 34" x 34". Designed and made by the author and machine quilted by Diane Ebner, Phoenix, Arizona. A nineteenth-century Jacquard coverlet was the inspiration for this quilt.

This quilt is the second in my series of quilts inspired by the beautiful woven coverlets made during the nineteenth century. Blue and white was probably the most popular choice for these coverlets, but red and white was certainly a close second. I took some liberty with my blue-and-white color combination and added just a touch of red.

BLUEWORK & BEYOND
Quilt size 34" x 34"

Supply List

1 yd. light background

½ yd. dark blue print for center medallion appliqué

½ yd. second dark blue print for side panel appliqué

¼ yd. third dark blue print for bird appliqué in the corner blocks

¼ yd. of red print for bird wings and binding

½ yd. light blue print for sashing and inner border

½ yd. fourth dark blue print for outer border

2 yds. lightweight, paper-backed fusible web

6 skeins DMC floss, blue 312

38" x 38" batting

38" x 38" backing

Cutting Measurements

I always cut my background a little larger than called for because the appliqué and stitching may shrink the background slightly. Trim the pieces to size after the stitching is complete.

Center block (light background)
1 square 16" x 16"

Side panels (light background)
4 rectangles 7" x 16"

Corner blocks (light background)
4 squares 7" x 7"

Sashing and inner border (light blue print)
2 strips 1" x 16"
4 strips 1" x 7"
4 strips 1" x 30"
2 strips 1" x 31"

Outer border (fourth dark blue print)
2 strips 2" x 31"
2 strips 2" x 34"

Binding (red print)
4 strips 1⅛" x 39"

Find It
Directions for Appliqué . . . . .page 9
Transferring Embroidery Designs . . . .page 10
Embroidery Stitches . . . . .page 12

Directions

1. Using fusible web, appliqué the BLUEWORK & BEYOND center medallion design on page 26 onto the center background block.

2. Embroider around the edges of the medallion with a buttonhole stitch sewn with two strands of embroidery floss.

3. Transfer the embroidery designs (page 27) to the medallion center and to the background of the center block. Embroider the designs with a stem stitch and two strands of floss.

4. Referring to the quilt photo on page 23, appliqué and embroider the designs on pages 28–29 to the side panels and the corner blocks as you did the center block.

5. After all the background pieces are completed, piece the quilt top together following the quilt layout shown in figure 13.

6. Refer to the Finishing Your Quilt section (pages 13–14) for further instructions on quilting, binding, and labeling your quilt.

Quilting Suggestions

BLUEWORK & BEYOND was machine quilted by my friend, Diane Ebner. She used a clear monofilament thread on the top and white thread in the bobbin. It is quilted in the ditch around the sashing and borders. The blocks are quilted in a 1" grid and stitched over the appliqué and the embroidery. The border is done in a meandering stitch.

Fig. 13. BLUEWORK & BEYOND **quilt layout**

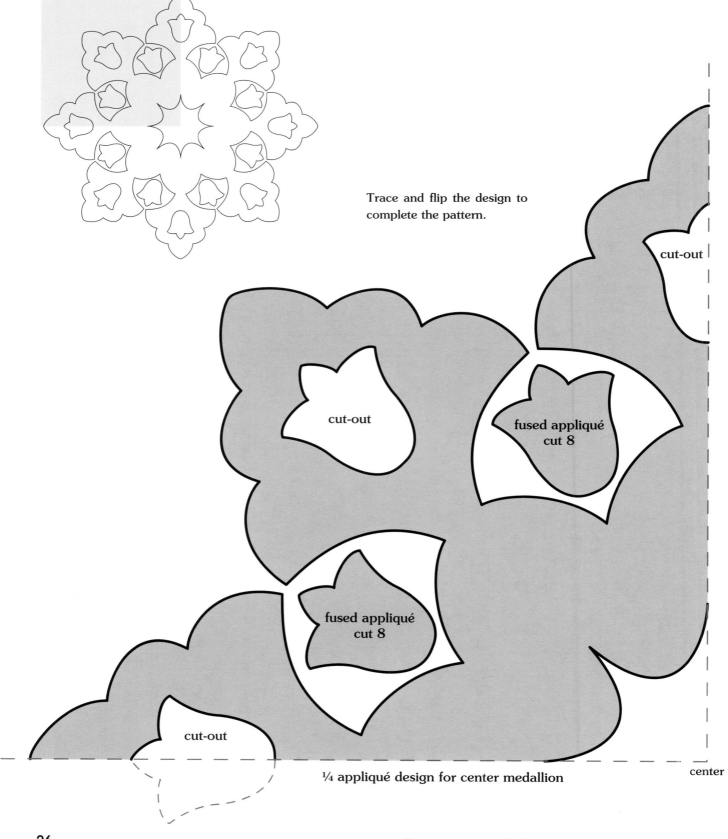

Trace and flip the design to
complete the pattern.

cut-out

cut-out

fused appliqué
cut 8

fused appliqué
cut 8

cut-out

¼ appliqué design for center medallion

center

embroidery design around
center medallion

Trace and flip to complete the pattern
around the center medallion.

embroidery design for
center medallion

If using fusible web, reverse and flip this design for opposite corners of the quilt.

½ side panel appliqué and embroidery

Trace and flip the design to
complete the pattern.

Cherry Berry Album

Appliqué and embroidery quilt, 50½" x 50½", designed and made by the author and machine quilted by Diane Ebner, Phoenix, Arizona. This quilt was based on traditional album quilts, but Betty introduced a funky twist.

Album quilts have been popular for more than 150 years. Each generation has put its own twist on this old favorite. Most of the blocks in this quilt were derived from appliqué seen on nineteenth century quilts. I chose designs that had a slightly funky look, added a bright new color scheme, and created my own version of a twenty-first century album quilt.

Cherry Berry Album
Quilt size 50½" x 50½"

Supply List

3 yds. light background for nine blocks, first and third border, and corner border squares

¼ yd. fabric for horizontal sashing

¾ yd. fabric for vertical sashing and second border fabric. (The second border can be cut selvage to selvage in one piece or cut lengthwise and pieced.)

An assortment of bright prints for the appliqué and sashing corners

½ yd. binding fabric, to be pieced

5 yds. lightweight, paper-backed fusible web

An assortment of embroidery floss that matches or contrasts with your fabric selection

55"x 55" batting

55"x 55" backing

Cutting Measurements

I always cut my background a little larger than called for because the appliqué and stitching may shrink the background slightly. Trim the pieces to size after the stitching is complete.

NOTE: When cutting background blocks, cut from the length of the fabric along one side, thus allowing enough length at the other side of the yardage for the borders.

Background
  9 blocks 12½" x 12½"

Horizontal sashing
  6 strips 1½" x 12½"

Vertical sashing
  18 strips 1½" x 12½"

Sashing corners (bright print)
  16 squares 1½" x 1½"

First border (light background)
  4 strips 2¼" x 40½"

Second border
  4 strips 2" x 40½"

Third border (light background)
  4 strips 2¼" x 40½"

Border corner blocks (light background)
  4 squares 5½" x 5½"

Binding fabric
  4 strips 1⅛" x 54"

Directions

1. Using fusible web, appliqué the CHERRY BERRY ALBUM block designs on pages 33–45 onto the background blocks.

2. Embroider around each appliqué piece with a buttonhole stitch and two strands of floss. You may use matching or contrasting thread, depending on the look you want to achieve.

3. Transfer the single lines in the designs onto the background and embroider them with a stem stitch. Use two strands of floss.

4. Press your completed blocks, and trim them to size if you cut them larger than called for in the cutting measurements. Lay out the blocks, using the photo of the quilt on page 30 as a guide.

5. Referring to the CHERRY BERRY ALBUM quilt layout (fig. 14), sew the sashing strips and the sashing corner set-squares to the appliqué blocks. The quilt photo on page 30 will help you to see where the sashings are placed.

6. Sew the first, second, and third borders together along their long edges. You should have four sets of borders.

7. Sew a border strip to the top and bottom of the quilt center.

8. Sew the border corner blocks to the short ends of the two remaining borders. Sew these borders to the sides of the quilt.

Fig. 14. CHERRY BERRY ALBUM quilt layout

9. Appliqué the corner motifs on this page to the border corner blocks, making sure there is at least ½" background beyond the design so that the binding will not cover it. Appliqué the flower design to the lower-left corner and the three butterfly motifs to the remaining corners. Notice that the butterflies at the top of the quilt face down, and the one at the bottom of the quilt faces upward.

10. After completing the appliqué on the corner blocks, use an extra-hard pencil to draw a line around the appliqué design, ¼" away from the appliqué and connecting to the second border. Refer to the Border Corner placement diagram (fig. 15). Buttonhole-stitch around the design on this drawn line, with two strands of floss.

11. Refer to the Finishing Your Quilt section (pages 13–14) for further instructions on quilting, binding, and labeling your quilt.

Quilting Suggestions

This quilt was machine quilted by Diane Ebner, with clear monofilament thread on top and white thread in the bobbin. It was quilted in the ditch between the blocks, sashing, and border strips. She quilted around each appliqué design and used a little free-form quilting in some of the larger areas of the appliqué pieces. The background was quilted in a meandering design.

corner motifs

Fig. 15. Border Corner placement

Row 1, block 1

Trace and flip the design around
the center to complete the pattern.

¼ pattern

center

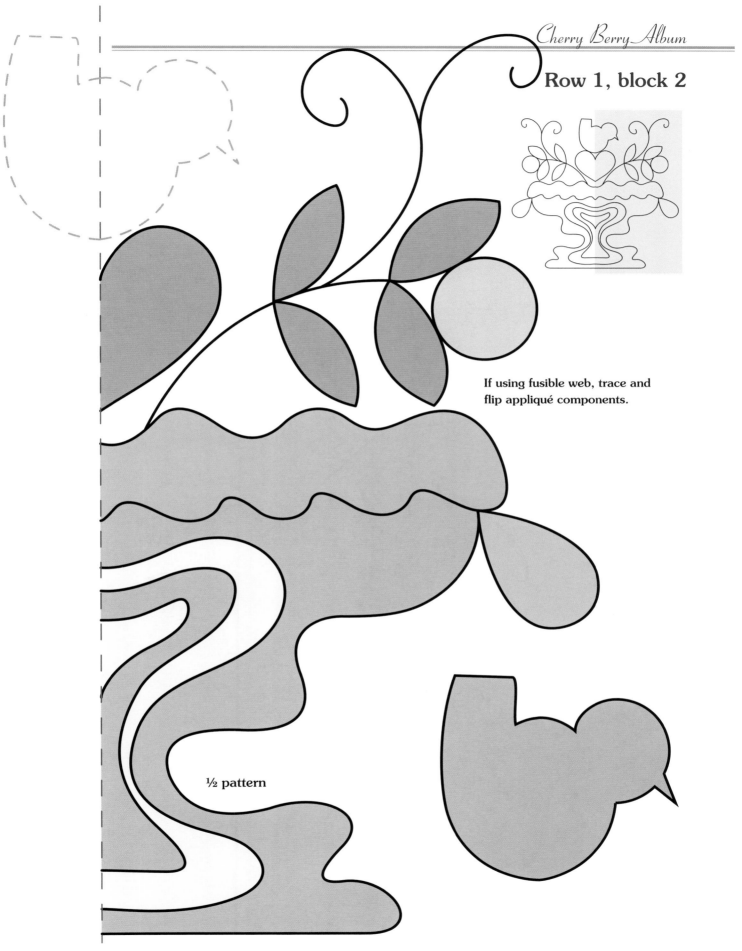

Row 1, block 2

If using fusible web, trace and flip appliqué components.

½ pattern

Row 1, block 3

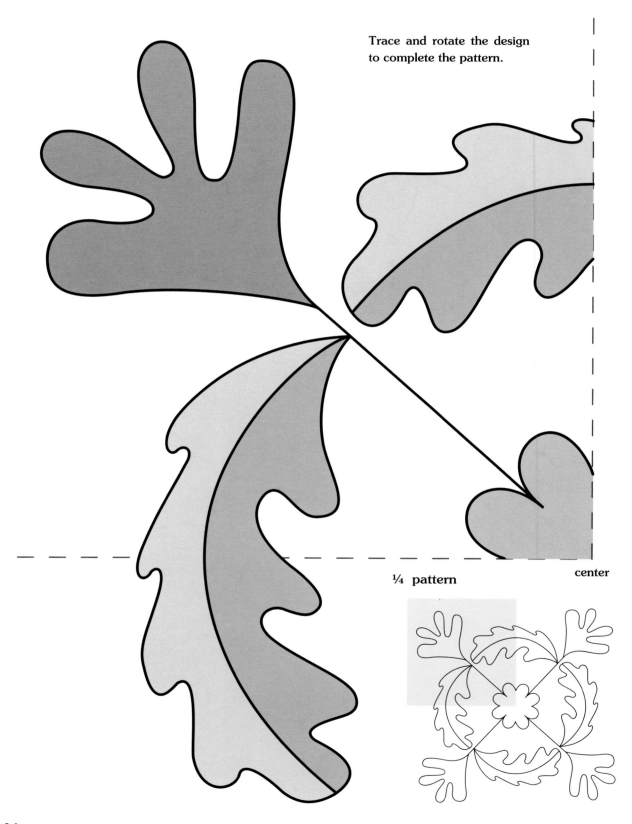

Trace and rotate the design
to complete the pattern.

¼ pattern   center

Row 2, block 2

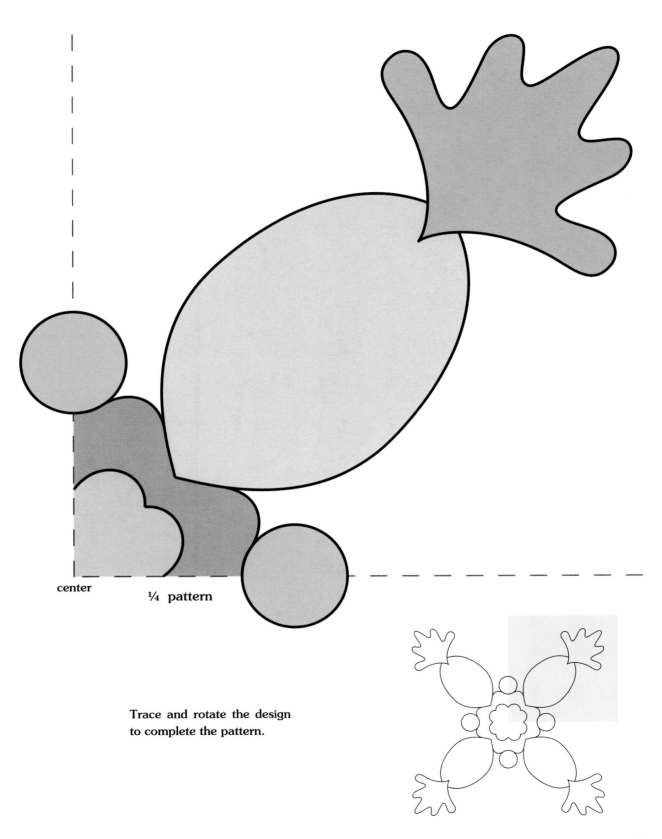

center

¼ pattern

Trace and rotate the design
to complete the pattern.

Row 2, block 1

If using fusible web, trace and flip appliqué components.

connect here

Row 2, block 1

connect here

Row 2, block 3

connect here

Row 2, block 3

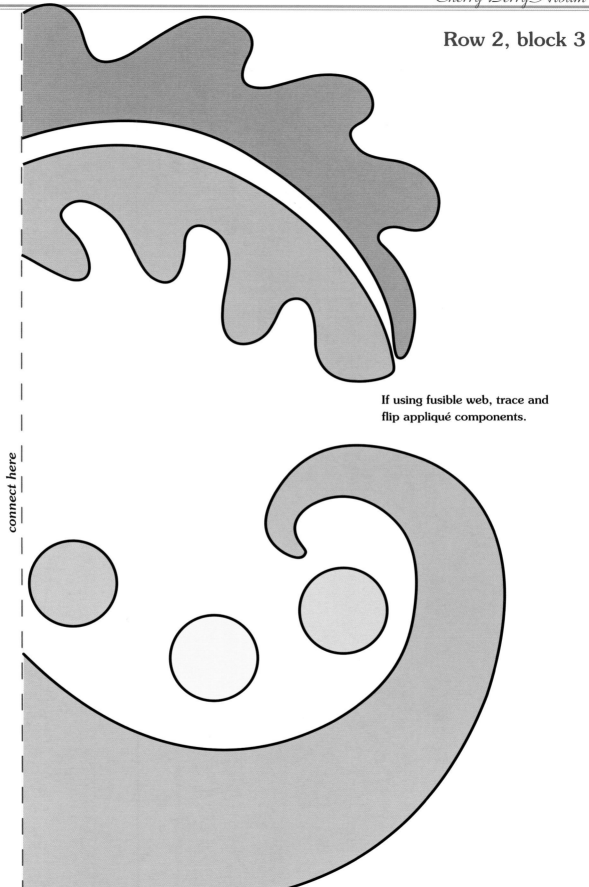

If using fusible web, trace and
flip appliqué components.

connect here

Row 3, block 1

Trace and flip the design to complete the pattern.

¼ pattern

center

Row 3, block 3

Trace and flip the design around the center heart to complete the pattern.

center

¼ pattern

Row 3, block 2

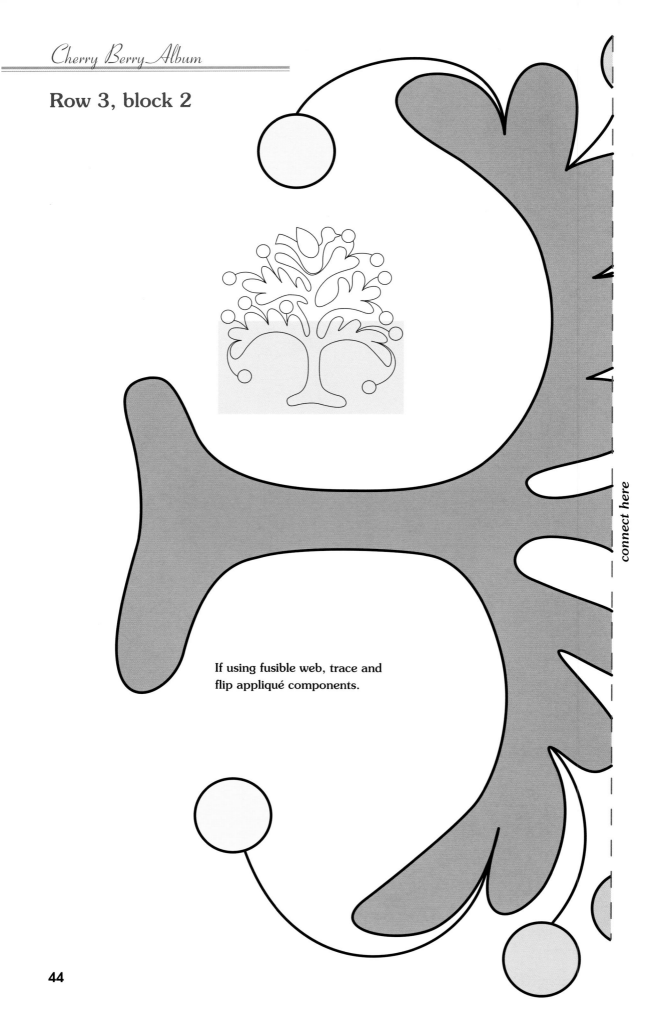

If using fusible web, trace and
flip appliqué components.

connect here

connect here

Funky Folk Art Redwork

*Appliqué and embroidery quilt, 35" x 35", designed and made by the author.
While based on traditional album quilts, Betty's designs have a stylish twist.*

Buttonhole stitching and red ombré embroidery floss add elements of surprise to this new version of vintage-style album quilts. The designs are slightly relaxed and funky, so I hope you will relax and enjoy making this fun quilt. I offer suggestions for the embroidery stitching, but perhaps you will think of some other creative ways of stitching the details.

FUNKY FOLK ART REDWORK
Quilt size 35" x 35"

Supply List

1 yd. light background

½ yd. sashing

1 yd. appliqué, corner set-squares, middle border, and binding fabric

¾ yd. print for inner and outer border

1½ yd. lightweight, paper-backed fusible web

4 skeins DMC floss: red ombré 115 or 75 (optional: red 498 or 321)

2 skeins DMC floss, ecru

39" x 39" batting

39" x 39" backing

Cutting Measurements

I always cut my background a little larger than called for because the appliqué and stitching may shrink the background slightly. Trim the pieces to size after the stitching is complete.

Background
9 squares 8½" x 8½"

Sashing
24 strips 1" x 8½"

Corner set-squares
16 squares 1" x 1"

Middle border
2 strips 1½" x 29½" for the top and bottom
2 strips 1½" x 31½" for the sides

Binding
4 strips 1⅛" x 40"

Inner border (print)
2 strips 2" x 26½" for the top and bottom
2 strips 2" x 29½" for the sides

Outer border (print)
2 strips 2½" x 31½" for the top and bottom
2 strips 2½" x 35½" for the sides

Directions

1. Using fusible web, appliqué the FUNKY FOLK ART REDWORK pieces (pages 49–57) to the background blocks.

2. Using two strands of ecru floss, buttonhole-stitch around the edges of the appliqué pieces.

3. Transfer the embroidery lines to the background blocks.

4. Using a buttonhole stitch and two strands of red ombré floss, embroider the traced designs. Where there is a single line, such as a stem, use the stem stitch or a running stitch.

5. After all the blocks are completed, assemble the quilt top according to the quilt layout shown in figure 16.

6. Refer to the Finishing Your Quilt section (pages 13–14) for further instructions on quilting, binding, and labeling your quilt.

Quilting Suggestions

This quilt was beautifully machine quilted by Diane Ebner. Using clear monofilament thread on the top and white thread in the bobbin, Diane quilted in the ditch between the borders. The center of the quilt was quilted in a 1" grid right over the appliqué, embroidery, and the sashing. The inner and outer borders were quilted in a meandering design.

Fig. 16. FUNKY FOLK ART REDWORK **quilt layout**

Row 1, block 1

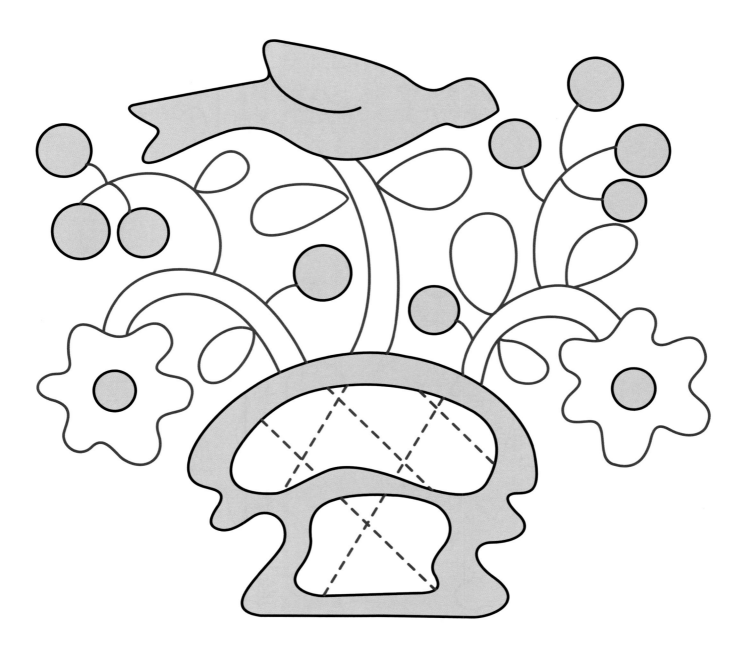

If using fusible web, trace and flip appliqué components.

Row 1, block 2

If using fusible web, trace and flip appliqué components.

Row 1, block 3

If using fusible web, trace and flip appliqué components.

Row 2, block 1

If using fusible web, trace and flip appliqué components.

Row 2, block 2

If using fusible web, trace and flip appliqué components.

Row 2, block 3

If using fusible web, trace and flip appliqué components.

Row 3, block 1

If using fusible web, trace and flip appliqué components.

Row 3, block 2

If using fusible web, trace and flip appliqué components.

Favorite Appliqué & Embroidery Quilts ~ Betty Alderman

Row 3, block 3

If using fusible web, trace and flip appliqué components.

Just My Doodles

Appliqué and embroidery quilt, 17½" x 19½", designed and made by the author

In the evening, when I am relaxing in front of the TV, I find that keeping a sketchbook close by is a good idea. It's surprising how many design ideas pop into my head when the television fare isn't too exciting. For some reason, unknown to me, I have started to enjoy drawing exotic, make-believe flowers and vines. Here is an example of one of the flowers that started to grow in my mind when I put pencil to paper and just started to doodle.

Just My Doodles
Quilt size 17½" x 19½"

Supply List
1 yd. light background for center block and outer borders

½ yd. solid green for appliqué and inner border and binding

¼ yd. solid red for appliqué

scraps of four different green prints

scrap of red print

scrap of solid yellow fabric

1 yd. lightweight, paper-backed fusible web

2 skeins of DMC floss, red 498

2 skeins of DMC floss, green 986

21" x 23" batting

21" x 23" backing

Cutting Measurements
I always cut my background a little larger than called for because the appliqué and stitching may shrink the background slightly. Trim the pieces to size after the stitching is complete.

Light background
1 rectangle 9½" x 11½" from light background

Inner border (solid green)
2 strips 1½" x 9½" for the top and bottom
2 strips 1½" x 13½" for the sides

Note: *It will be easier to appliqué and embroider the outer borders before they are cut into strips. See step 4 on page 60.*

Outer border (light background)
2 strips 3½" x 11½" for the top and bottom
2 strips 3½" x 19½" for the sides

Binding (solid green)
2 strips 1⅛" x 22"
2 strips 1⅛" x 24"

Directions

1. Using fusible web, fuse the JUST MY DOODLES appliqué pieces on pages 61–63 to the background block. Refer to the quilt photo on page 58 for fabric placement.

2. Using two strands of floss and matching the thread to the fabric, buttonhole-stitch around the appliqué pieces. The yellow circle is stitched in red.

3. Transfer the embroidery lines to the background. Embroider these lines with a stem stitch or buttonhole stitch, as indicated on the pattern.

4. With a pencil, lightly outline the border measurements onto the light background fabric. Before you cut out the borders, appliqué and embroider the border strips in the same manner as for the center block. Cut the border strips.

5. Assemble the quilt as shown in the quilt layout in figure 17.

6. Refer to the Finishing Your Quilt section (pages 13–14) for further instructions on quilting, binding, and labeling your quilt.

Quilting Suggestions

Hand quilting helps set off the vines and designs within this little quilt. The background of the center block is quilted in a 1" grid. The appliqué has been quilted around the outside edges. In the outer border the quilting is done ¼" from the appliqué and the vines. In some of the more open spaces it is echo quilted. The edges of the green inner border are quilted in the ditch.

Fig. 17. JUST MY DOODLES **quilt layout**

buttonhole stitch

If using fusible web, trace and flip appliqué components.

connect here

satin stitch

connect here

**appliqué and embroidery designs
for short border (top and bottom)**

If using fusible web, trace and flip appliqué components.

satin stitch

connect here

appliqué and embroidery designs
for long border (sides)

May Basket

Appliqué and embroidery quilt, approximately 20" x 20", designed and made by the author

The single block in this quilt is quite versatile. It can stand alone as in this little quilt, or making multiples of this block and placing them in other settings, such as in A "Touch" of Home or Blue Tulips, will create distinctly different looking quilts. The lovely floral fabric in the outside border sets the stage for the colorway of this little quilt. Pink, lavender, green, and, yes, even orange, were just some of the colors considered for the rest of the quilt. I urge you to raid your button box for the finishing touches. You can make it in a weekend!

May Basket
Quilt size 20" x 20"

Supply List

NOTE: There are two sets of borders in this quilt. The set around the center block consists of two borders called the center block inner and outer borders. The set of three borders around the outside of the entire quilt is referred to as the inner, middle, and outer borders.

- ½ yd. white-on-white for background and triangles

- ¼ yd. for center block, inner border, and appliqué

- ⅛ yd. for center block outer border

- ¼ yd. for quilt inner border and appliqué

- ¼ yd. for quilt middle border and appliqué

- ⅝ yd. for quilt outer border and binding

- Additional scraps for appliqué

- Several skeins of embroidery floss in colors that complement your fabrics

- 1 yd. lightweight, paper-backed fusible web

- 12 buttons for embellishment

- 24" x 24" batting

- 24" x 24" backing

Cutting Measurements

I always cut my background a little larger than called for because the appliqué and stitching may shrink the background slightly. Trim the pieces to size after the stitching is complete.

Background
1 block 8½" x 8½"

Background triangles
2 squares 9" x 9" cut once diagonally to form 4 half-square triangles (fig. 18)

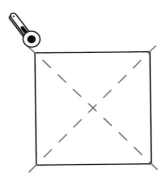

Fig. 18. Cutting for background triangles

Center block, inner border
    2 strips 1¼" x 8½"
    2 strips 1¼" x 10"

Center block, outer border
    2 strips 1¼" x 10"
    2 strips, 1¼" x 11½"

NOTE: *See steps 6 through 10 on page 67 to determine the length of the quilt inner, middle, and outer borders.*

Binding fabric
    4 strips 1⅛" x 25"

Directions

1. Using fusible web, appliqué the MAY BASKET patterns (pages 68–69) onto the background of the center block.

2. Using two strands of floss, buttonhole-stitch around the appliqué.

3. Transfer the embroidery detail onto the background of the center block and the basket. With a stem stitch and two strands of floss, complete the embroidery on the center block.

4. Apply the inner and outer center block borders. Refer to the MAY BASKET quilt layout (fig. 19).

Fig. 19. MAY BASKET **quilt layout**

5. Stitch the long edge of each background triangle to the edges of the center block. Trim the edges of the triangles so that the seam allowance is ¼" beyond the point of the block borders (fig. 20).

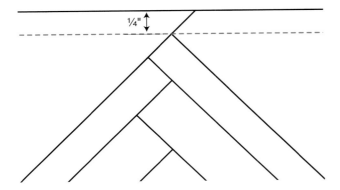

Fig 20. Seam allowance

6. Measure the width of the center block, including the center block borders.

7. Cut two strips of the inner border fabric, 1" wide by the width of the center. Stitch these two borders to the top and bottom of the quilt center.

8. Now measure the length of the quilt center, plus the two added borders to determine the length of the two remaining inner border strips. Cut these borders strips and stitch them to the sides of the quilt center.

9. Measuring as before, cut the middle border strip 1¼" wide by the required length and sew them to the quilt center.

10. Add the outside border strips, cutting them 1½" wide by the required length, in the same manner as for the two previous borders.

11. Fuse and appliqué the leaf motifs on page 69 to the triangles. Refer to the quilt photo on page 64 for placement. Buttonhole-stitch around the leaf motifs with two strands of floss.

12. Transfer the embroidery detail to the triangles. Complete the embroidery detail with a running stitch and two strands of floss.

13. Refer to the Finishing Your Quilt section (pages 13–14) for further instructions on quilting, binding, and labeling your quilt.

14. After your quilting is complete, you may want to add a few buttons for embellishment. Refer to the quilt photo on page 64 for placement.

Quilting Suggestions

I used clear monofilament thread to machine quilt in the ditch between all the borders. It is also quilted around each appliqué motif and near the embroidery detail in the triangles. The outside floral border is machine quilted in a meandering pattern.

If using fusible web, trace and flip appliqué components.

appliqué pattern
for corner triangles

Blue Tulips

Machine appliqué and hand embroidery quilt, 41" x 41", designed and made by the author

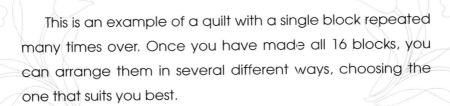

This is an example of a quilt with a single block repeated many times over. Once you have made all 16 blocks, you can arrange them in several different ways, choosing the one that suits you best.

BLUE TULIPS
Quilt size 41" x41"

Supply List

NOTE: Yardage is based on fabric that is at least 40" wide. Borders are cut from the length of the fabric, parallel to the selvages.

1⅜ yd. light background

1⅜ yd. pale blue for stem and leaf appliqué, and the inner and outer border fabric

1⅜ yd. pale green for stem and leaf appliqué and binding

1¼ yd. bright blue for tulip appliqué and middle border

⅛ yd. purple for inner tulip appliqué

3 yds. lightweight paper-backed, fusible web

2 skeins DMC floss, blue 312

Thread to match fabrics for machine appliqué

45" x 45" batting

45" x 45" backing

Cutting Measurements

I always cut my background a little larger than called for because the appliqué and stitching may shrink the background slightly. Trim the pieces to size after the stitching is complete.

Background (light background)
16 blocks 9" x 9"

Inner border (pale blue)
4 strips 1" x 43"

Middle border (bright blue)
4 strips 2" x 43"

Outer border (pale blue)
4 strips 2" x 43"

Binding (pale green)
4 strips 1⅛" x 46"

Directions

1. Using fusible web, appliqué the BLUE TULIP designs on page 73 onto the background blocks. Refer to the quilt photo on page 70 for color guidance. *Note: The butterfly design is to be embroidered onto four of the blocks.*

2. With your sewing machine set at a narrow buttonhole or zigzag stitch and using thread to match the fabric, stitch around each appliqué piece. Note: This is a good time to put on a good audio book. By the end of the day you will have accomplished two very worthwhile things.

3. Trace the butterfly design onto four of the blocks. Embroider the butterflies with a buttonhole stitch and two strands of floss.

4. Lay out the 16 blocks, placing the four embroidered butterfly blocks in the center, with the butterflies facing outward.

5. Stitch the 16 blocks together, according to the quilt layout shown in figure 19 and the photo on page 70.

6. Sew the inner, middle, and outer border strips together along their long edges. You should have four sets of borders. Center the borders on the edges of the quilt center. Stitch to within ¼" of the ends of the quilt.

7. Miter the corners according to your method of choice, or refer to the directions for Mitered Corners on page 19.

8. Refer to the Finishing Your Quilt section (pages 13–14) for further instructions on quilting, binding, and labeling your quilt.

Quilting Suggestions

This quilt was hand quilted around each appliqué piece and again ¼" beyond that. The butterflies were traced onto the outside blocks and quilted. The rest of the quilt was then echo quilted.

Fig. 19. BLUE TULIPS **quilt layout variation**

Rotate blocks as shown in
figure 19 on page 72.

A "Touch" of Home

Appliqué and embroidery quilt, 32" x 32", designed and made by the author

As I was working on this quilt, my thoughts were often of my mother. In some way this quilt reminds me of her and my childhood home. When my daughter saw the quilt for the first time she said, "It reminds me of Grandma." The name comes from the fact that my mother's maiden name was Touchstone, and she and her brothers and sisters were often nicknamed "Touch."

A "Touch" of Home
Quilt size 32" x 32"

Supply List

NOTE: *Yardage is based on fabric that is at least 40" wide. Borders to be mitered are cut parallel to the selvage edge.*

- 1 yd. light background for four center blocks and appliquéd border

- ½ yd. medium green for inner border, binding, and leaf appliqué

- ½ yd. pink and green print for third border

- ¾ yd. light green for outside border and leaf appliqué

- Scraps of one red, two more greens, three pinks, one blue, and one yellow for appliqué

- 2 yds. lightweight, paper-backed fusible web

- 3 skeins DMC floss, green 3052

- 1 skein each of the following DMC floss (or colors of your choice):
  Red 498
  Blue 311
  Yellow 3855
  Pink 604

- 36" x 36" batting

- 36" x 36" backing

Cutting Measurements

I always cut my background a little larger than called for because the appliqué and stitching may shrink the background slightly. Trim the pieces to size after the stitching is complete.

Background (light background)
   4 squares 9" x 9"

Inner border (medium green)
   2 strips 1¼" x 17½" for top and bottom
   2 strips 1¼" x 19" for sides

Appliquéd border (light background)
   4 strips 4" x 30" Note: These borders are mitered.

Third border (pink and green print)
   2 strips 1½" x 26" for the top and bottom
   2 strips 1½" x 28" for the sides

Outside border (light green)
   2 strips 3" x 28" for the top and bottom
   2 strips 3" x 32" for the sides

Binding (medium green)
   4 strips 37" x 1⅛"

Directions

1. Using fusible web and the buttonhole stitch, appliqué the A "TOUCH" OF HOME designs (pages 77–78) onto the background blocks. Match the embroidery floss to the fabrics.

2. Transfer the embroidery lines onto the blocks. With a stem stitch and two strands of green floss, complete the embroidery on each block.

3. Center and appliqué four border designs (page 77) onto each of the light background border strips. Do not appliqué the corner blue flowers at this time. Complete the embroidery on the borders.

4. Referring to the quilt layout shown in figure 20, stitch the four center blocks together.

5. Apply the top and bottom inner borders to the quilt center. Then, sew the side inner borders to the quilt center.

6. Add the appliqué borders next, mitering the corners according to your method of choice, or refer to the directions for Mitered Corners on page 19.

7. Appliqué the blue flowers to the four corners of the appliqué border. See the photo of the quilt on page 74 for proper placement.

8. Apply the third border and the outer border as you did the inner border.

9. Refer to the Finishing Your Quilt section (pages 13–14) for further instructions on quilting, binding, and labeling your quilt.

Fig 20. A "TOUCH" OF HOME **quilt layout**

Quilting Suggestions

This quilt was quilted by hand. Using white quilting thread, I quilted in the ditch around the blocks and borders. I quilted close to each appliqué piece and then again ¼" from the appliqué. Using green quilting thread, I quilted the outer border in a free-form loop-de-loop design. If you are not comfortable drawing a free-form design, I would suggest using one of the beautiful border templates available.

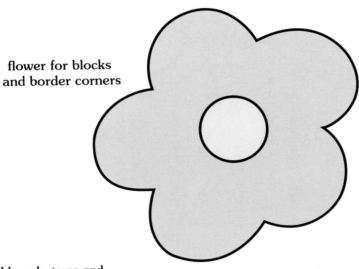

flower for blocks and border corners

If using fusible web, trace and flip appliqué components.

border element

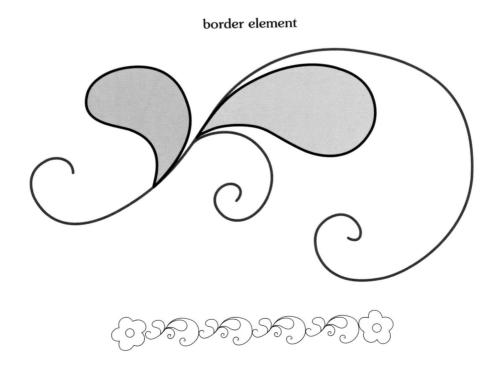

If using fusible web, trace and flip appliqué components.

Rotate blocks as shown in figure 20 on page 76.

Crazy for Bluework

Crazy quilt with bluework embroidery, 39½" x 39½", designed and made by the author

Crazy quilts have been popular in America since the late 1870s. They were often made up of silks and velvets and showcased the maker's talent for elaborate embroidery. They probably were never meant to be bed coverings, but were surely displayed prominently in the parlor, draped over the piano or sofa.

This crazy quilt features a different bluework design in each block. It is made of the contemporary cotton prints that we so love to collect today, rather than the silks and velvets of the past.

CRAZY FOR BLUEWORK
Quilt size 39½" x 39½"

Supply List

24 different blue and yellow prints for piecing the crazy quilt blocks and for corner blocks (Prints should range from light to dark.)

1 yd. solid, light background fabric for the embroidery

¾ yd. border fabric (cut crosswise)

¼ yd. binding fabric

2 skeins each of DMC floss: blue 791, 792, 793. Note: Each embroidery design is worked in three shades of blue.

44" x 44" batting

44" x 44" backing

Cutting Measurements

I always cut my background a little larger than called for because the appliqué and stitching may shrink the background slightly. Trim the pieces to size after the stitching is complete.

Embroidery background
9 squares 10" x 10"

Border
4 strips 3½" x 33½"

Corner blocks
4 blocks 3½" x 3½" from different prints

Binding
4 strips 1⅛" x 44"

Directions

1. Transfer each of the nine embroidery designs (pages 83–85) onto the background squares by the method you prefer.

2. Embroider the designs with two strands of floss. Use all three shades of blue in each design. It doesn't matter where you use each shade, but using all three will give added dimension to your work. Press the finished embroidery squares face down on a well-padded surface.

3. Making an irregular five-edged shape, cut away the excess fabric around the embroidery design, as shown in figure 21. Be sure to leave a 1" margin beyond the embroidery.

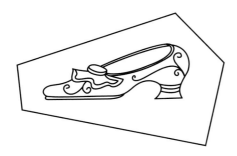

Fig. 21. Cut away excess fabric around the embroidery design.

4. With right sides together, place your first scrap of print fabric along one edge of the embroidered piece. Stitch along this edge (fig. 22).

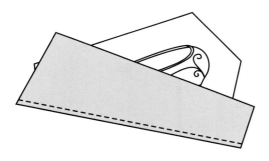

Fig. 22. Place and stitch the first print.

5. Flip the print scrap back and press. Trim away the excess print fabric to make a straight edge (fig. 23).

6. Add another scrap to the new edge in the same manner as for the first scrap (fig. 24). Continue adding scraps around the embroidered center until you have a piece large enough to trim into an 11½" x 11½" square block.

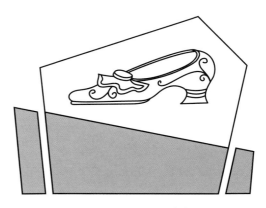

Fig. 23. Trim away the excess fabric.

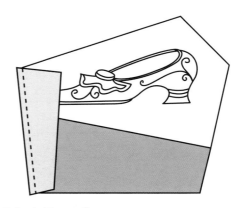

Fig. 24. Add another scrap.

7. With two strands of blue floss, sew a running stitch around the inside edge of the embroidered section of the block (fig. 25).

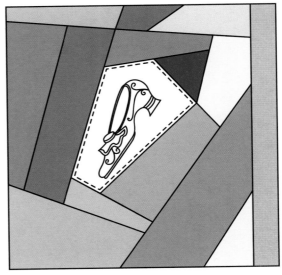

Fig. 25. Sew a running stitch around the inside edge.

8. Make all nine blocks in the same manner. Piece the nine blocks together following the quilt layout shown in figure 26.

9. Sew a corner block to each end of the of the two side border strips.

10. Apply the top and bottom borders. Assemble the rest of the quilt as shown in the quilt layout.

11. Refer to the Finishing Your Quilt section (pages 13–14) for further instructions on quilting, binding, and labeling your quilt.

Quilting Suggestions

I hand quilted ¼" away from the edges of the embroidered pieces in each block. This is the only quilting there is on the light background of the embroidery. I machine quilted the rest of the quilt, stitching in the ditch between each block and along the border. The rest of the quilt was machine quilted in a meandering design.

Fig. 26. CRAZY FOR BLUEWORK **quilt layout**

French knot

satin stitch

embroidery motifs

satin stitch

embroidery motifs

embroidery motifs

Hearts & Flowers

Redwork wallhanging, 19½" x 40½", designed and made by the author

Here is a wallhanging that can be hung year around, but I think it would be especially fitting for Valentine's Day. The background of the redwork and the outside border incorporate the use of linen-blend fabrics. Jumbo rickrack plays a part, too. The rickrack seems to set off the two floral prints that have been placed next to each other as borders.

HEARTS AND FLOWERS
Quilt size: 19½" x 40½"

Supply List

⅜ yd. light colored linen-like or linen-blend fabric for redwork background

NOTE: All borders are cut selvage to selvage.

¼ yd. red-and-white check for borders around each block

½ yd. floral for sashing and first border

⅜ yd. linen-blend or home-decorating floral fabric for the second border. This fabric should be similar in color to the floral fabric used in the sashing and first border.

¼ yd. solid red for the binding

4 yds. jumbo red rickrack

4 skeins of DMC floss, red 498

24" x 45" batting

24" x 45" backing

Cutting Measurements

I always cut my background a little larger than called for because the appliqué and stitching may shrink the background slightly. Trim the pieces to size after the stitching is complete.

Background
3 rectangles 9½" x 8½"

Borders around each block (check)
12 strips 1" x 9½"

Sashing and first border (floral)
4 strips 2½" x 10½"
2 strips 2½" x 35½"

Outer border (linen floral)
2 strips 3" x 14½"
2 strips 3" x 40½"

Binding (solid red)
2 strips 1⅛" x 24"
2 strips 1⅛" x 45½"

Directions

1. Transfer the embroidery designs (pages 89–91) onto the linen background blocks. Note: When transferring a design onto linen-type fabric, you may need to use a red permanent pen and a light box.

2. Using a stem stitch and two strands of floss, embroider the floral designs within the hearts.

3. Buttonhole-stitch the scalloped heart borders. Press your completed blocks.

4. Referring to the HEARTS AND FLOWERS quilt layout (fig. 27), sew six of the check strips to the long edges of the embroidered blocks.

5. Sew the remaining check strips to the sides of the embroidered blocks.

6. Add the sashing strips and the first border strips to the embroidered blocks. Sew the top and bottom linen floral borders onto the quilt center, inserting the rickrack into the seam.

7. Sew the two linen floral side borders onto the long edges of the quilt, inserting the rickrack into the seam.

8. Refer to the Finishing Your Quilt section (pages 13–14) for further instructions on quilting, binding, and labeling your quilt.

Quilting Suggestions

This wallhanging was quilted around the hearts and the scalloped heart borders with ecru DMC Pearl Cotton, size 12. Using the same thread, it was quilted in the ditch between the borders and through the center of the sashing and the first border. Red DMC Pearl Cotton, size 12, was used to quilt through the center of the outer border.

Fig. 27. HEARTS AND FLOWERS **quilt layout**

Top block

Bottom block

Bonus pattern

The Apron Brigade

THE APRON BRIGADE place mats, 11" x 13", designed and made by the author

These little place mats are just a tease to get you started in creating all sorts of wonderful projects. Try your hand at transferring a drawing or photos onto fabric, using your scanner or a color copier and some colored pencils or crayons. In this fun project you will experiment with using pretreated fabric sheets that you can purchase at your quilt shop.

THE APRON BRIGADE PLACE MAT
Place mat size: 11" x 13"

Supply List

Colored pencils or crayons

Small amounts of coordinating print fabrics for place mat borders

13" x 15" cotton batting for each place mat

11½" x 13½" backing for each place mat

Fine line permanent pen, black or brown

Paper-backed, pretreated fabric sheets (See the Sources section on page 94.)

Plain copy paper

Ink-jet color printer, scanner, and computer or color copier (You can have the color copies done at a copy center.)

Directions

1. Using a fine line pen, copy or trace THE APRON BRIGADE design for place mats (this page) onto a sheet of copy paper. Enlarge 400%.

2. Using colored pencils or crayons, color the design. The more creative you are with the coloring, the better your design will look when copied. The more dense your colors, the better they copy.

3. Using either the scanner or a color copier, scan or copy your colored picture onto the specially treated fabric sheet. Trim your fabric color copy to measure 8½" x 7½".

4. Border your fabric color copy with several strips of coordinating print fabrics, cut into random widths, until your piece measures 11½" x 13½". Refer to the photo of the place mats on page 92.

5. Layer the batting, place mat top, and backing by placing the batting on the bottom, the place mat top in the middle, face up, and the backing on top, face down.

6. Using a ¼" seam allowance, stitch around the outside edge of all three layers, leaving a 4" opening on one edge. Trim away the excess batting and turn right side out.

7. Whipstitch the opening closed as shown on page 13.

8. Quilt the three layers together by hand or machine.

THE APRON BRIGADE place mat pattern. Enlarge 400% at a copy center.

Sources

Fabric sheets for ink-jet printers are available at most full service quilt shops, including Bernina Connection LIC, 4219 East Indian School Rd., Phoenix, AZ 85018. 602-553-8350.

Suggested Reading

Anderson, Clarita S. *American Coverlets and Their Weavers.* Athens, Ohio: Ohio University Press, 2002.

Cheney, Joyce. *Aprons, Icons of the American Home.* Philadelphia and London: Running Press, 2000.

Hargrave, Harriet. *Mastering Machine Appliqué.* Lafayette, CA: C&T Publishing, Inc., 2002.

Montano, Judith Baker. *Elegant Stitches.* Lafayette, CA: C&T Publishing, Inc.,1995.

Smith, Lois Tornquist. *Fun & Fancy Machine Quiltmaking.* Paducah, KY: American Quilter's Society, 1989.

About the Author

Betty Alderman has been designing patterns for quilts since 1992. With a background in fine arts and a lifelong love of sewing, quilt designing seems to suit her perfectly. She markets her patterns under the name Betty Alderman Designs.

In addition to teaching at guilds around the country, Betty is a quilt collector. She enjoys speaking about her antique quilts, imparting interesting facts and stories about her collection.

When she is not busy with her quilt design business or traveling to a teaching engagement, Betty is at home with her husband, Fred. While they will testify that the New York summers are delightful, Betty and Fred try to enjoy a little sunshine during the winter months by traveling south in their motor home.

other AQS books

This is only a small selection of the books available from the American Quilter's Society. AQS books are known worldwide for timely topics, clear writing, beautiful color photos, and accurate illustrations and patterns. The following books are available from your local bookseller, quilt shop, or public library.

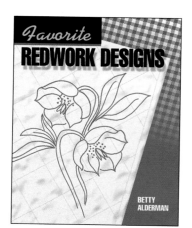

#5331   us$16.95

#6205   us$24.95

#6008   us$19.95

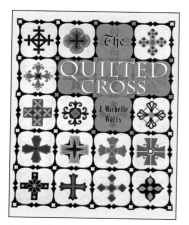

#6301   us$18.95

#6407   us$21.95

#6292   us$24.95

#6300   us$24.95

#6211   us$19.95

#5763   us$21.95

LOOK *for these books nationally.* **CALL** **1-800-626-5420**
or **VISIT** our Web site at **www.AQSquilt.com**